Klara Balthasar

Special Relationships. Anglo-American Stereotypes in Nancy Meyer's Film "The Holiday"

GRIN Publishing

Bibliographic information published by the German National Library:

The German National Library lists this publication in the National Bibliography; detailed bibliographic data are available on the Internet at http://dnb.dnb.de .

Imprint:

Copyright © 2009 GRIN Verlag GmbH
Print and binding: Books on Demand GmbH, Norderstedt Germany
ISBN: 978-3-656-84703-8

This book at GRIN:

http://www.grin.com/en/e-book/284413/special-relationships-anglo-american-stereotypes-in-nancy-meyer-s-film

GRIN - Your knowledge has value

Since its foundation in 1998, GRIN has specialized in publishing academic texts by students, college teachers and other academics as e-book and printed book. The website www.grin.com is an ideal platform for presenting term papers, final papers, scientific essays, dissertations and specialist books.

Visit us on the internet:

http://www.grin.com/

http://www.facebook.com/grincom

http://www.twitter.com/grin_com

Special Relationships -

Anglo-American Stereotypes in Nancy Meyers' Film
The Holiday

Table of Contents

1. Introduction

"The house exchange confirms our most improbable visions of how the other side of the pond lives"[1]

The Holiday is a romantic comedy that tells the story of two women who change their love lives by changing their homes. However, this paper does not deal with amorous involvements and personal happy endings; it aims to analyse the various Anglo-American stereotypes that are used in the film and what they can tell us about the special relationship between the USA and the UK.

In order to do so, some general information about the film and its historic context will be given. Following this, there will be a short plot summary. Then, the paper will examine which Anglo-American stereotypes are displayed by the characters and the settings. To end with, two major cultural differences between the USA and the UK will be discussed.

2. About the Film

2.1. General Information

The Holiday is a romantic comedy which was released in 2006. The screenplay was written by Nancy Meyers, an American director, producer and screenplay writer, who also directed the film. The movie is starring Kate Winslet, Cameron Diaz, Jude Law and Jack Black. It won the Teen Choice Award 2007 and was nominated for several other prizes, including the ALMA Award 2007 and the NRJ Cinè Award 2007.[2]

2.2. Historic Context

In 2006, the relationship between the USA and the UK was not at its best. It was the third year of the war in Iraq and the fifth year of the rather special relationship between Britain's Prime Minister Tony Blair and the President of the United States George W. Bush. While the Americans appreciated the British as valuable support in the war, the British people strongly disliked the close relationship to the USA and felt that Tony Blair presented himself as Bush's poodle. In a *Times* poll, 65% of the British sample "agreed that Britain's future lies more with Europe than with America" and only 44% of the participants agreed that "America is a force for good in the world"[3]. A *Guardian/ICM* poll found out that 63% of the British think that Blair "has tied Britain too closely to

---

1 Carina Chocano,"The Holiday". *Los Angeles Times* (12/8/2006) found at
http://www.calendarlive.com/printedition/calendar/cl-et-holiday8dec08,0,2932207.story.
2 Found at http://www.imdb.com/title/tt0457939/awards.
3 Found at http://www.populuslimited.com/the-times-political-attitudes-040606.html.

the US"[4].

Although the film was released in 2006 and has a contemporary setting, it does not give any clues regarding the difficult relationship between the USA and the UK in these times. It rather focuses on interpersonal relationships than on political or economic issues.

2.3. Plot summary

The centrepiece of the movie is a home exchange between two women: Amanda Woods (Cameron Diaz), owner of a prosperous film trailer company in Los Angeles and Iris Simpkins (Kate Winslet), a sentimental wedding columnist for *The Daily Telegraph* in London. They both are stuck in their (love) lives. Amanda just found out that her boyfriend Ethan (Edward Burns) has been cheating on her while Iris has been suffering from an unrequited love for her colleague Jasper (Rufus Sewell) for several years. As the Christmas holidays are close, they decide that they need some time off and look for possibilities to get away. Finally, they meet on a home exchange website and spontaneously agree to switch houses.

Amanda moves into Iris' small country cottage in Surrey, while Iris enjoys the comfort of Amanda's extravagant mansion in Los Angeles and luxuriates in her surroundings. In the meantime, Amanda has some difficulties in her new environment. After six hours in England, she even plans to get the next flight back home. But then she meets Iris' handsome brother Graham (Jude Law) and they spend a passionate night together. Amanda decides to stay and during her holidays she gets to know Graham better. She discovers that he is not only a charming British gentleman, but also a widower and father of two little girls. Eventually, they fall in love with each other and become a couple.

Across the Atlantic, Iris makes new acquaintances, too. She befriends Miles Dumont (Jack Black), a soundtrack composer and Arthur Abbott (Eli Wallach), an elderly man from the neighbourhood. It turns out that Arthur has been one of the most successful screenplay writers during Hollywood's Golden Age. Iris and Miles help him to prepare for an award ceremony. In the course of the film, Iris and Miles get closer and - after Miles has discovered that his girlfriend Maggie has been cheating on him – become a couple.

The last scene shows the two new couples and Graham's children happily celebrating New Year's Eve together in Surrey.

---

4 Julian Glover, Ewen MacAskill, "Stand up to US, voters tell Blair". *The Guardian* (7/25/2006) found at http://www.guardian.co.uk/politics/2006/jul/25/uk.topstories3.

3. Anglo-American Stereotypes in the Film – Characters and Setting

In general, there are two kinds of stereotype depending on the point of view: Auto-stereotypes and hetero-stereotypes. Auto-stereotypes describe "the way in which a group perceives itself"[5] while hetero-stereotypes describe "the way a certain group sees another group"[6]. As the screenplay writer, Nancy Meyers, is American, I consider the stereotypes about the British as hetero-stereotypes and the stereotypes about the Americans as auto-stereotypes.

In order to analyse which Anglo-American stereotypes have been used in *The Holiday*, it is important to have a look at the characters and the settings. The characters reveal how the Americans and the British are seen in the film, while the settings show how the two countries are portrayed.

3.1. The American Characters

In *The Holiday*, there are three major American characters: Amanda Woods, Miles Dumont and Arthur Abbott. They are quite different from each other, but they all represent various stereotypical aspects of being an American.

3.1.1. Amanda Woods

Amanda Woods represents a stereotypical American in various ways. First of all, she is a self-made woman and probably also a self-made millionaire. She owns a prospering company that produces trailers for Hollywood films and definitely loves her job. Working comes first in Amanda's life. Her boyfriend Ethan thinks that she works too much as she "cut 75 trailers this year, put a cutting room in the house and [...] sleep[s] with [her] BlackBerry"[7]. Amanda herself is convinced that one has to stay professional no matter what is happening in one's personal life[8], even if this means that you have no time for sex.[9]

In her job, she is paid "the big bucks"[10] and thus can afford some luxury in her life, which points to the stereotype of the materialistic American. According to the 'Xenophobe's Guide to the Americans' "Americans think of everything in terms of money because money can be quantified. In the game of life, money is the most effective way to keep score"[11].

---

5 Stephan-Alexander Ditze, *America and the Americans in Postwar British Fiction: An Imagological Study of Selected Novels,* (Heidelberg: 2006) 33.

6 Ibid.

7 *Liebe braucht keine Ferien*, written by Meyers, Nancy. Directed by Meyers, Nancy. Produced by Block, Bruce A.; Farwell, Suzanne; Meyers, Nancy. 2006. DVD. Waverly Films Production. 2006. DVD. 0:12:03.

8 Cf. Ibid. 0:15:41.

9 Cf. Ibid. 0:15:41.

10 Ibid. 0:16:10.

11 Stephanie Faul, *Xenophobe's Guide to the Americans* (London: Oval Books, 2009) 14.

The dark side of Amanda's job is the severe stress she suffers from. She is under permanent pressure and seems to be hyperactive. There is also a hint that Amanda even suffers from workaholism: In important situations, she hears a voice that comments her life like a trailer narrator.[12] Due to all this and her emotional situation, she thinks that she might "need some peace and quiet or whatever it is people go away for"[13]. However, instead of relaxing and enjoying the tranquillity of her new English surroundings, she becomes frustrated and massively bored as soon as she cannot busy herself[14]. This permanent need to be occupied or entertained is another American stereotype.

The fear of not being busy the whole time might stand for the fear of thinking about one's life and dealing with personal problems. Amanda probably is a workaholic because she wants to divert herself from her insecurity in matters of personal relationships and emotions. She is troubled by intimacy and, according to Ethan, she "screw[ed] up every relationship [she's] ever been in"[15], which seems to be a stereotypical behaviour pattern for an American as they have are afraid of permanent commitments[16]. She cannot show her true feelings and tends to push people away when they get too close. When she is on her first date with Graham, she cannot relax and simply be herself, but instead interrogates him as if he was applying for a job[17]. Since her parents got divorced when Amanda was fifteen years old, she has never been able to cry again.[18] Sometimes she makes attempts, but she never succeeds[19]. Instead of showing real emotions in stressful situations, she suffers from oesophageal spasms[20]. Amanda's strategy of hiding her true emotions and her insecurity is stereotypically American, too, as "being depressed is unattractive and thus not suitable for public display"[21].

Another area Amanda is not comfortable with is her sexuality. She appears to be very straightforward and open about it when she offers Graham a one-night-stand[22]. However, immediately after he consents, she tells him that she is "not very good at this"[23]. So, although Amanda is very open about sex she is not relaxed and very insecure. A problem, many Americans seem to suffer from as whatever kind of sex they're having, Americans know that

---

12 Cf. *Liebe braucht keine Ferien*, DVD.0: 25:23.
13 Ibid. 0:16:24.
14 Cf. *Liebe braucht keine Ferien*, DVD 0: 30:05 and 0:32:26.
15 Cf. Ibid. 0:12:44.
16 Cf. "Indeed, permanent commitments are what Americans fear the most" in Faul, *Xenophobe's Guide to the Americans*, 1.
17 Cf. Ibid 1:03:23.
18 Cf. Ibid. 1:05:27.
19 Cf. Ibid. 0:18:29.
20 Cf. Ibid. 0:13:37.
21 Faul, *Xenophobe's Guide to the Americans*, 10.
22 Cf. *Liebe braucht keine Ferien*, DVD. 0:44:20. "I'm thinking we should have sex. If you want".
23 *Liebe braucht keine Ferien*, DVD. 0:45:05.

it could be better. Books about improving one's sex life top the sales charts, and women's magazines in particular feature at least one 'How to Have Better Sex' article every month. Nowadays, it's OK to be open about sex. But being open isn't the same thing as being relaxed.[24]

Another feature Amanda is constantly occupied with is her outer appearance. She is always dressed very elegantly. Being tall, slim and blond, she is very attractive and embodies the perfect American woman: Barbie[25]. Amanda's attitude towards food, however, shows which sacrifices American women have to make in order to get the perfect shape. They cannot eat carbohydrates without wanting to kill themselves[26] and they have to "approach every meal mindful that the food will either be bad for them or, worse, make them fat"[27].

All in all, Amanda Woods represents different facets of the stereotypical American: She embodies the materialistic yuppie culture and the beauty craze.

But Amanda changes during her holiday in England. Although she is bored at first and would rather go home as soon as possible, she stays and starts to become a more relaxed person. In Graham, she finds a person who is really interested in her and allows her to open up and be herself again. The absence of diversion in her vacation spot makes her re-evaluate her life and she manages to have real emotions again, symbolised by her crying in the end. The trailer narrator's voice comments this development as follows: "Amanda Woods, welcome back"[28].

3.1.2. Miles Dumont

Miles Dumont differs largely from Amanda, but he also embodies aspects of a stereotypical American. As a soundtrack composer, he works in the superficial world of Hollywood and seems to be totally absorbed by his environment as he only talks about films and soundtracks. The superficiality of the film industry seems to have rubbed off on him, too. His relationship with Maggie, an actress, does not have a base of common interests or tender feelings. All Miles ever says about his girlfriend is that she is very beautiful.[29] Maggie is not interested in Miles at all; she only enjoys his admiration and probably hopes to benefit from his contacts in the film industry. Thus, Miles does not only live in a superficial world, he is also superficial himself and judges people by their surface. So, Miles represents the stereotypically superficial American, to whom the outer

---

24 Faul, *Xenophobe's Guide to the Americans*, 28.
25 Cf. *Liebe braucht keine Ferien*, DVD. 1:16:09. "You look like my Barbie"
26 Ibid. 0:16:47.
27 Faul, *Xenophobe's Guide to the Americans*, 55.
28 *Liebe braucht keine Ferien*, DVD 2:02:34.
29 Cf. Ibid. 1:10:37.

appearance is more important than character attributes.

Another American stereotype Miles stands for is America-centricity. Miles has, like so many other Americans, never been to Europe[30] and he probably has never been interested in going there either. Iris has noticed his America-centricity, too, as she says "Can't believe he'd ever come over here"[31], when he is visiting her in England for New Year's Eve. Miles does not only see the United States as the centre of the world, he also seems to look down on the rest of the world. Although it was probably meant to be a joke, Miles' remark that there is a parcel "from a little town called London, England"[32] tells the spectator that he indeed thinks of London as a little town and that one has to clarify which London is meant: London, USA or London, England.

Miles' behaviour in public is stereotypically American, too. The 'Xenophobe's Guide to the Americans' says that "Americans are like children: noisy, curious, unable to keep a secret, not given to subtlety, and prone to misbehave in public"[33]. This is a very exact description of Miles' behaviour. He sometimes is embarrassingly direct in his utterances. For example, when he accidentally brushes Iris' breast in a restaurant, he does not just politely ignore it or apologise discreetly. Instead, he very loudly says "Sorry about that. Boob graze. That was accidental. Accidental boob graze"[34] and thus makes the whole situation even more awkward. He is also very noisy and seems to enjoy misbehaving in public. When he accompanies Iris to the video store, he starts to sing out very loudly different soundtracks. When he notices Iris' embarrassment he just says "It's not a library. I can go loud"[35].

Miles' attitude to his body differs greatly from Amanda's body-awareness. His body represents the stereotype of the chubby American. Miles does not worry about eating carbohydrates; if anything, he enjoys the "best drink in town"[36], which consists of chocolate, ice cream and a lot of whipped cream and seems to be a product of Starbucks. Thus, he also embodies the stereotype of the overweight American fast-food consumer.

Still, Miles does not only embody negative American stereotypes. His openness and his ability to adapt are stereotypically American features, which are due to the United States' status as a country of immigrants. Americans have learnt to adopt features, products and rituals of various cultures. In *The Holiday*, the Jewish culture represents the influence of different cultures in the USA. Miles is very open about celebrating a Hanukah-party at Iris' place and he even displays

---

30 Cf. Faul, *Xenophobe's Guide to the Americans*, 3.
31 *Liebe braucht keine Ferien*, DVD. 2:04:10.
32 Ibid. 1:09:00.
33 Faul, *Xenophobe's Guide to the Americans*, 1.
34 *Liebe braucht keine Ferien*, DVD. 1:45:05.
35 Ibid. 1:31:27.
36 *Liebe braucht keine Ferien*, DVD. 1:29:14.

knowledge about the Jewish culture, as he uses many Yiddish words, for example "I can play spin the dreidel"[37].

During the movie, Miles succeeds in leaving some of his rather negative stereotypical characteristics behind: The acquaintance (and later also the relationship) with Iris helps him to expand his horizon: He learns to look behind the surface of people and he acknowledges that there is a world beyond America; At New Year's Eve, he even sets off to discover good old Europe, which is rather new to him.

3.1.3. Arthur Abbott

Arthur Abbott is Iris' elderly neighbour in Los Angeles. He embodies yet further stereotypical aspects of being an American.

First of all, Arthur represents the American Dream and the Golden Age of Hollywood. When he was seventeen years old, Arthur first worked as a messenger for the Western Union and then as Louis B. Mayer's office boy[38]. From there, he became a very successful screenplay writer, got to work with Hollywood icons like Cary Grant and even won an Academy Award.[39] His career is an example of a successful realisation of the American Dream.

His age and the frailty of his body, however, symbolise that his personal American dream as well as the Golden Age of Hollywood will soon come to an end. Arthur is aware of that development and heavily criticises the recent development in Hollywood. He is against the solely capitalistic interests of the film industry, the sheer abundance of films and the resulting decline of quality[40].

Apart from his role in Hollywood's film industry, Arthur as a Jew represents the melting-pot or salad-bowl ideal of the USA. The spectator does not come to know whether Arthur is an immigrant or whether his family has been American for generations. But the spectator does learn that Arthur has made it in the USA and feels American, while he is also able to uphold the Jewish culture at the same time.

3.2. The British Characters

In *The Holiday* there are two major British characters: Iris Simpkins and her older brother Graham Simpkins. To find distinctly British features in these characters was more difficult than finding stereotypically American features in their American counterparts. This might be due to the fact that the screenplay writer herself is American and thus might have examined her fellow

---

37 Ibid. 1:09:34.
38 Cf. *Ibid.* 0:58:00.
39 Cf. *Liebe braucht keine Ferien.* DVD. 0:54:53 and 0:56:41.
40 Cf. Ibid. 1:25:00.

compatriots more closely and more critically.

3.2.1. Iris Simpkins

Iris is a wedding columnist for 'The Daily Telegraph' in London. This fact is highly ironic because she has been suffering from an unrequited love for her colleague Jasper Bloom for over three years. She wants to fall out of love with him, but she does not succeed because Jasper is engaging her further, although he plans to marry a different woman.

Although her emotional situation is very distressing, Iris is determined to keep her composure. At the Christmas Party in the office she is worried about her colleagues seeing her cry[41] because to a British person "creating a scene in public is altogether unacceptable"[42]. Iris is definitely a very sensitive person, but she is also in charge of her emotions: She waits until she is at home where no one can see her before she starts to cry for days[43].

Further character features of Iris are her courteous behaviour[44] towards Arthur and her articulateness[45] in every situation.

Once, she shows a stereotypically British behaviour when she makes a cup of tea for Miles after he found out that his girlfriend has cheated on him[46]. Here, the spectator learns that the English indeed "have imbued tea with almost mystical curative and comforting qualities"[47].

During her holiday in Los Angeles, Iris develops from "a lovesick English rose"[48] into the leading lady of her own life. She stops being composed in every situation and finally manages to stand up to Jasper and tell him that it is finally over. This gain of gumption could be due to her Californian surroundings, because

> [u]nderneath [...] calm exterior [of the British] [...] there seethes a
> primitive unruliness which they have never quite been able to
> master. Climate has a lot to do with it. Heat waves bring out the
> beast in the English. Cold and drizzle calm them down.[49]

So, one could argue that Iris' development in California is a stereotypical for British people, who are suddenly exposed to the sun.

---

41 Cf. *Liebe braucht keine Ferien*, DVD. 0:04:15. "Does it look like I'm crying right now?" .

42 Antony Miall, David Milsted, *Xenophobe's Guide to the British* (London: Oval Books, 2009) 12.

43 Cf. *Liebe braucht keine Ferien*, DVD. 0:10:22.

44 Cf. Ibid. 0:54:06. "Can I offer you a lift home?".

45 Cf. Ibid. 1:36:00.

46 Cf. Ibid. 1:32:43.

47 Miall, Milsted, *Xenophobe's Guide to the British*, 42.

48 Manohla Dargis, "Changing Addresses, Altering Love Lives". *The New York Times* (12/8/2006) found at
http://movies.nytimes.com/2006/12/08/movies/08holi.html?ref=movies.

49 Miall, Milsted, *Xenophobe's Guide to the British*, 13.

3.2.2. Graham Simpkins

Graham Simpkins is Iris' older brother. He is a widowed book editor and father of two girls. When he is free of any parental or vocational obligations, he frequents the local pub, which – of course - can be evaluated as a stereotypically British behaviour pattern. One might even assume that he has a drinking problem.[50]

A more positive British stereotype that is applicable to Graham is that of the British Gentleman. Graham is very courteous and articulate and likes to pay compliments, even when he is drunk.

A rather Un-British trait is that he is given and used to one-night-stands[51]. Thus, it is not very surprising that he immediately consents when Amanda, a total stranger to him, suggests having sex. Still, he seems to be taken aback by Amanda's directness[52] as British women usually deal differently with sexual matters.

The spectator furthermore learns that Graham has a cow in his backyard and sews[53]. He also admits that he is "a major weeper"[54], like his sister Iris. To me, these features do not at all appear to represent stereotypically British ways. Nancy Meyers probably used them in order to stress the opposites between Americans and the British.

At the beginning of the film, Graham is an overcharged and confused widower with a drinking problem, who, nonetheless, is a good father to his children. The relationship with Amanda helps him to balance his life and de-compartmentalise[55] it again.

3.3. The Setting

This part analyses how the USA and the UK are depicted in the film. The setting is twofold: first, there are distinct regions of the countries and second, there are the houses of Amanda and Iris which need to be considered.

3.3.1. California

Nancy Meyers has not only chosen her home state in order to represent the USA in *The Holiday*. She has also picked a state that is like no other because of "its size, diversity [and] power"[56] and "the state that represents the greatest distance to the Old World, both geographically

---

50 Cf. *Liebe braucht keine Ferien*, DVD. 0:40:21 "Unfortunately, it has become a bit of a routine".
51 Cf. Ibid.0:43:15.
52 Cf. Ibid. 0:49:09. "Well, utter honesty".
53 Cf. Ibid. 1:24:00.
54 Ibid. 1:06:10.
55 Ibid. 1:21:25.
56 Stephen Fry, *Stephen Fry in America* (London: Harper,2009) 308.

11

and culturally"[57].

The choice of California also represents some stereotypes about America. First, it is the home of Hollywood and thus the home of superficiality, too. As J.G. Ballard says in *Hello America*:

> [...] Hollywood [...] project[s] a fictional image of America far more powerful than the reality. Whenever I visit the United States I often feel that the real "America" lies not in the streets of Manhattan and Chicago, or the farm towns of the mid-west, but in the imaginary America created by Hollywood and the media landscape.[58]

According to this, Hollywood is and produces what (Non-) Americans perceive as the real America.

Secondly, Nancy Meyers' California seems to be the fulfilment of the American Dream. Everything is just perfect: There are only rich, successful people living in big beautiful houses, driving around in big cars. The weather is nice and warm, the plants are green and lush and you see the Sunset Boulevard and summery beaches. Even the wind – the Santa Anas – seems to be part of the American way of life and the American firm belief that everything is possible, as "when the Santa Anas blow, all bets are off. Anything can happen"[59].

3.3.2. Amanda's Mansion

Amanda's mansion fits perfectly into the scheme: It is immensely big and beautiful. Its furnishing is very elegant and modern and confirms Amanda's sense for style. In the house you find everything one could possibly desire: a big kitchen, a spacious office, a fitness room, a double king-size bed and a large swimming pool. The office and the cutting room in the house confirm the stereotype of the workaholic; the fitness room and the swimming pool hint at the Americans' need to constantly improve their bodies and their personal fitness.

Despite all the comfort and luxury, the house resembles a museum. There are no personal things lying around and its size ensures that its inhabitants have enough (or maybe too much) personal space. Amanda's mansion is beautiful, but it is also the opposite of a homely and cosy place.

3.3.3. Surrey

The portrayal of England in *The Holiday* probably fulfils all stereotypes Americans might have about Great Britain. Big Cities do not appear[60] as Iris lives in "Shere, a quaint village in the

---

57 M. Hünemörder, B. Waldschmidt-Nelson, M. Zwingenberger, *Europe and America: Cultures in* Translation (Heidelberg: Winter, 2006) Preface.

58 J .G.Ballard, *Hello America* (London:1994) Introduction.

59 *Liebe braucht keine Ferien*, DVD. 0:36:00.

60 Cf. *Liebe braucht keine Ferien*, DVD. London is only mentioned once and the spectator gets a glimpse of the Houses of Parliament (0:09:24).

countryside [of Surrey] that dates back to the 11th century"[61] The picture is characterised by a romantic pastoral landscape, tiny villages and old buildings. Everything seems to be very idyllic; there are sheep everywhere and sometimes one even hears church bells ringing. The ancient buildings and the beautiful manor where Amanda and Graham have their first proper date symbolise England's rich history and tradition.[62]

Another stereotypical - and at the same time authentic - part of the British setting is the local pub. Pubs have been a community institution[63] in England for centuries and they are an inherent part of British culture. Graham is a frequent visitor of the local pub; Amanda joins him one night, drinking more than she ever has before in her life[64], which is probably due to the British custom of drinking rounds[65].

One aspect of Britain has always been and is still subject of every English stereotype: The bad weather. In *The Holiday*, the English weather is the opposite of the nice and warm climate in California. It is freezing cold and wintery snowy; the weather forecast says that "[m]ost of northern England [...] will have sleet and snow in the morning and again later in the day"[66]. However, the cold weather just underlines the snugness of the pub and of Iris' small cottage.

3.3.4. Iris' Cottage

Iris' cottage is the epitome of British cosiness. It is very small and "looks as if it has been drawn by Beatrix Potter"[67]. Iris describes her house as "fairy tale English cottage set in a tranquil country garden [...] [and a]n enchanting oasis of tranquillity in a quiet English hamlet"[68]. This description and the fact that her little cottage has a name[69] assert the stereotype that an Englishman's home is his castle[70].

The furnishings are rather old-fashioned and lack comfort: There is a fireplace, a gas cooker and a boiler. Still, everything appears to be very snug and homely.

Iris' dog Charlie seems to feel quite at home at Rosehill Cottage, too, and he verifies the stereotype that "[a]nimals, especially pets, are vital to English life"[71].

---

61 Official movie website, to be found at http://www.sonypictures.com/movies/theholiday/site/main.html.

62 Cf. *Liebe braucht keine Ferien*, DVD . 0:26:40, 1:02:37 and 1:03:00.

63 Miall, Milsted, *Xenophobe's Guide to the British*, 61.

64 Cf. *Liebe braucht keine Ferien*, DVD. 1:00:10 "I haven't had that much to drink in—Oh, what am I saying? I've never had that much to drink.".

65 Miall, Milsted, *Xenophobe's Guide to the British*, 61.

66 *Liebe braucht keine Ferien*, DVD. 0:31:35.

67 Manohla Dargis, "Changing Addresses, Altering Love Lives".*The New York Times*(12/8/2006).

68 *Liebe braucht keine Ferien*, DVD. 0:19:15.

69 Cf. ibid. 0:09:56. "Rosehill Cottage".

70 Miall, Milsted, *Xenophobe's Guide to the British*, 39.

71 *Liebe braucht keine Ferien*, DVD. 0:19:41.

All in all, the American and the English setting reveal further Anglo-American stereotypes and form an immediate contrast between luxurious magnitude and homely cosiness.

4. Anglo-American Contrasts

Apart from different Anglo-American stereotypes that are displayed in *The Holiday*, there are also two major Anglo-American contrasts, which should be discussed. The first one is the contrast between Hollywood's film industry and England's literary tradition. The second contrast lies between modernity and tradition.

4.1. Hollywood's Film Industry vs. England's Literary Tradition

The contrast between Hollywood's film industry and England's literary tradition already becomes obvious during the first moments of the film. The first image the spectator sees is Miles composing a soundtrack; the first thing the audience hears is Iris quoting Shakespeare[72].

This separation between the USA and England becomes even more evident if you take a look at the occupations of the characters. All American protagonists have jobs in Hollywood's film industry while all English protagonists (including Iris' and Graham's parents) are occupied with literature and language in some way. Iris works as a columnist for *The Daily Telegraph*, Graham is a book editor, their father writes historical fiction and their mother is an editor at Random House.

The significance of literature or films respectively is also displayed in the furnishing of the protagonists' houses: While Iris' and Graham's house both contain loads of books, Amanda owns a big DVD collection and an appropriate home cinema.

The spectator probably also notices the extraordinary articulateness of both Iris and Graham. The American characters – Miles in particular – seem to be rather inarticulate in comparison to them. For example, after Iris' well-phrased monologue concerning the woes of unrequited love, Miles only replies "Well, fuck"[73].

Thus, to the English literature and language are very important and a natural part of their lives; the American equivalent is the world of films.

Arthur embodies a compromise between those two positions, as he is a screenplay writer and thus combines both worlds in his profession. Amanda intends to bridge the gap, too, as she plans to "read a book, not just a magazine [, a]n actual book"[74] when she is in England.

4.2. Modernity vs. Tradition

---

72 Cf.Ibid. 0:00:48 and 0:01:10.
73 *Liebe braucht keine Ferien*, DVD. 1:36:00.
74 Ibid. 1:16:49.

The second major difference between the United States and England is the contrast between modernity and tradition. The Americans, on the one hand, love modernity and everything that comes with it: new technologies, more comfort and more style. They live in a world of constant progress and it is their philosophy in life to always go on. The British, on the other hand, have a stereotypical need for tradition as it "represents continuity, which must be preserved at all costs"[75] to them.

In the film, these different attitudes become obvious when you consider the different kinds of equipment in the houses. Amanda's mansion is provided with the most modern technology: an automatic gate, automatic shutters in the bedroom and a gigantic television system.

Iris, who is not used to such state-of-the-art devices, reacts rather overwhelmed and says "Oh, that's intense"[76]. Her little cottage contains a far more rustic furnishing. It has a fireplace, a small bathtub and a boiler, as well as a gas cooker. Amanda is not too thrilled about the lack of comfort and comments her surroundings with an "OK, that'll be interesting"[77].

The last aspect which underlines the stereotype of the tradition-loving British pertains road traffic. To Amanda, the British left-hand traffic means that she has to "drive on the wrong side of the road [a]nd the wrong side of the car"[78]. To the British, however, "[d]riving on the left is traditional and therefore [...] indisputably best"[79].

5. Conclusion

To sum up, *The Holiday* contains many Anglo-American stereotypes. On the one hand, the Americans are depicted as being superficial and materialistic workaholics who cannot behave properly in public, who ignore the world that lies beyond America and who are either victims of the beauty craze or chubby fast-food consumers. California and the fake world of Hollywood represent the country they live in: Everything is big, beautiful, comfortable, modern and simply perfect. The British, on the other hand, are portrayed as composed, articulate and tradition-loving tea drinkers. They live in cosy cottages in a pastoral landscape surrounded by sheep and frequent the local pub in their leisure time. The film also displays major cultural contrasts between the two nations: In America, Hollywood's film industry and modernity are very important values, while England cherishes her literary history and tradition. All in all, the spectator gets a picture of two completely different countries and people.

However, when these two cultures clash due to the home exchange, only positive developments

---

75 Miall, Milsted, *Xenophobe's Guide to the British*, 35.
76 *Liebe braucht keine Ferien*, DVD. 0:34:13.
77 Ibid. 0:29:36.
78 Ibid.0:30:10.
79 Miall, Milsted, *Xenophobe's Guide to the British*, 68.

take place. After getting used to the new and totally different surrounding, Amanda, the American Barbie, and Iris, the English rose, magically find what has been missing in their lives. Amanda needed some peace and quiet in order to relax and refocus her life, whereas Iris required some gumption in order to move on.

So, the intended message of the film probably is that one can always learn from each other, no matter how big the differences are. With regard to the special relationship between the USA and the UK, the conclusion is that they are two very distinct nations that complement each other perfectly despite all dissimilarities.

For all the harmony, the spectator still notices that the point of view is American: the big gap in matters of comfort and technology between the USA and the UK assure the (American) audience that they live in an advanced high-tech culture while the English still have a cow in the backyard.

6. Bibliography

Primary Sources

Liebe braucht keine Ferien, written by Meyers, Nancy. Directed by Meyers, Nancy. Produced by Block, Bruce A.; Farwell, Suzanne; Meyers, Nancy. 2006. DVD. Waverly Films Production. 2006.

Secondary Sources

Ballard, J.G. *Hello America.* London: 1994.

Chocano, Carina. "The Holiday". *Los Angeles Times* (12/8/2006) (found at http://www.calendarlive.com/printedition/calendar/cl-et-holiday8dec08,0,2932207.story).

Dargis, Manohla. "Changing Addresses, Altering Love Lives". *The New York Times* (12/8/2006) (found at http://movies.nytimes.com/2006/12/08/movies/08holi.html?ref=movies).

Ditze, Stephan-Alexander. *America and the Americans in Postwar British Fiction: An Imagological Study of Selected Novels.* Heidelberg: Winter, 2006.

Faul, Stephanie. *Xenophobe's Guide to the Americans.* London: Oval Books, 2009.

Fry, Stephen. *Stephen Fry in America.* London: Harper, 2009.

Glover, Julian & MacAskill, Ewen."Stand up to US, Voters Tell Blair". *The Guardian* (7/25/2006) (Found at http://www.guardian.co.uk/politics/2006/jul/25/uk.topstories3)

Hünemörder, Markus & Waldschmidt-Nelson, Britta & Zwingenberger, Meike. „Preface". *Europe and America: Cultures in Translation.* Ed. Hünemörder, Markus and Waldschmidt-Nelson, Britta and Zwingenberger, Meike. Heidelberg: Winter, 2006.

Miall, Antony & Milsted, David. *Xenophobe's Guide to the British.* London: Oval Books, 2009.

Official movie website, found at http://www.sonypictures.com/movies/theholiday/site/main.html.

Poll found at http://www.populuslimited.com/the-times-political-attitudes-040606.html.

http://www.imdb.com/title/tt0457939/awards.